Who Was H. J. Heinz?

by Michael Burgan

illustrated by Stephen Marchesi

Penguin Workshop

Dedicated to all my nieces and nephews—MB

PENGUIN WORKSHOP
An Imprint of Penguin Random House LLC, New York

Visit us online at www.penguinrandomhouse.com.

Library of Congress Cataloging-in-Publication Data is available upon request.

ISBN 9780448488653 (paperback)   10 9 8 7 6 5 4 3 2 1
ISBN 9781524790950 (library binding)   10 9 8 7 6 5 4 3 2 1

Contents

Who Was H. J. Heinz? 1

The Young Salesman 5

Early Success 17

Starting Over 31

Seeds of Success 41

Building a Modern Company 51

"57 Varieties" and Many More 73

The Fight for Pure Food 84

Final Years 95

Timelines 104

Bibliography 106

Who Was H. J. Heinz?

In the summer of 1853, the people of Sharpsburg, Pennsylvania, often saw young Henry John Heinz strolling the village streets. He carried a basket in each hand filled with vegetables from his family's garden. Henry picked vegetables in the garden before and after he went to school. He would take whatever produce his family didn't need and sell it to his neighbors.

Henry enjoyed bringing fresh food to the village, and he was good at selling. By the time he was ten, he needed a wheelbarrow to carry all the vegetables he offered for sale. Two years later, his little business had grown so much that Henry used a horse to pull a cart filled with food.

From the beginning, he sold the freshest, best-tasting products. Henry wanted his customers to know that any food he delivered was worth the money they spent for it. And people grew to trust the Heinz name.

From that simple start, Henry built one of the largest food companies in the world. He moved his growing company to Pittsburgh. There, he built factories that used the most modern methods possible to process and package food. He also thought up new ways to attract customers' attention. One was to come up with a slogan—a phrase that described his company and its products. Henry put the slogan "57 Varieties" on all his labels. It let people know that Henry sold a wide range of products, from pickles to baked beans.

Selling food might seem like an easy thing to do. Everyone has to eat, and many people don't have time to raise crops and prepare their own foods. But H. J. Heinz made better-quality food and sold more of it than anyone else of his day. His hard work and smart ideas proved one of his favorite sayings: "To do a common thing uncommonly well brings success."

CHAPTER 1
The Young Salesman

Beginning in the 1680s, many German immigrants took the long voyage across the Atlantic Ocean to Pennsylvania. John Heinz made that trip in 1840, settling just outside of Pittsburgh in the village of Birmingham. The village sat along the Monongahela (say: muh-nah-guh-HEE-lah) River. The area was known for its bustling factories that made glass, iron, and bricks. The sky was often thick with smoke from the coal that was burned to power all the factory machines.

John Heinz found a job making bricks, and three years after his arrival in Birmingham, he met and married Anna Schmitt. Like her husband, she had come to Pennsylvania from Germany.

On October 11, 1844, the Heinzes had their first child, a boy they named Henry John but sometimes called Harry. The Heinz family would grow to include nine children: four boys and five girls. One of their daughters, however, died when she was only a baby.

The Heinzes lived in Birmingham until Henry was five years old, and then they moved to the nearby village of Sharpsburg. The town was on the banks of the Allegheny River and was famous for its brickyards. Mr. Heinz decided to go into the brickmaking business for himself.

Mrs. Heinz and the other German women in their community made most of their own food.

They grew many of the same crops they had in Germany, such as cauliflower, cabbage, potatoes, turnips, and carrots. The German families usually raised some chickens, too.

Mrs. Heinz was a deeply religious woman. She made sure all her children went to church, and she taught them lessons from the Bible. The Heinz family followed the Lutheran faith, and Henry went to a school run by a Lutheran church. He learned to read and write English, and did well in math. Every day he walked over a mile each way to school and back. Like many German immigrants, Mr. and Mrs. Heinz believed in the importance of hard work. They made sure Henry learned that, too.

By the time he was eight, Henry was working in the family garden before and after school. Then he started his own little business selling vegetables to neighbors. But that wasn't his only job. At times, he led the horses that pulled boats up the Allegheny River.

In the 1850s, small boats didn't have motors so they needed horsepower—horses walking along the riverbank, tied to the boats to pull them

along. Henry also picked potatoes for a local farmer. Years later, someone asked him how he could do so much at such a young age. He said simply, "We country boys work."

But selling vegetables was the job Henry liked
best. His parents saw that he was good at it, so
they gave him a small plot of the family's land.
Henry began raising his own crops to sell. And

when he was twelve, his little farm tripled in size. Henry bought a horse and cart to carry all his vegetables into town.

At fifteen, Henry quit school and began working for his father. But he decided to take just one more class, to learn bookkeeping. He wanted to learn how to keep track of the money his father's company spent on supplies and how much it earned selling bricks. Henry could use his bookkeeping skills in his own business, too.

And Henry's food business was expanding. At times, he awoke at 3:00 a.m. so he could take his vegetables to stores in Pittsburgh before going to work for his father. Henry also sold one product that came in a bottle—horseradish. Henry had

helped his mother prepare horseradish for their own family. And it wasn't a fun job. Horseradish grows as a root, so farmers have to dig it up, wash it, and then grate it.

Henry first made his horseradish in a brick home his father built for the family in 1854. (Henry had actually helped his father make some of the bricks for the house!) Because preparing

horseradish was hard work, Henry knew he could make money selling it to people who didn't want to bother making it themselves.

Henry also knew that other merchants sold their horseradish in dark bottles. They tried to cheat their customers by adding other things like leaves or wood pulp to the horseradish. And the dark glass bottles hid all those "add-ins."

The Tradition of Pickling Foods

Horseradish is made from the root of a plant in the mustard family. It is sharp and bitter-tasting. But once grated and pickled with salt and vinegar, horseradish root is used as a kind of relish with many other foods. It is just one of many vegetables that are pickled in the German tradition.

The word *pickle* comes from the Dutch *pekel* or Northern German *pökel*, meaning *salt* or *brine*, two important ingredients in the pickling process. Pickled cabbage is *sauerkraut* and pickled cauliflower is known as *chowchow*. And, of course, pickled cucumbers are simply *pickles.*

Henry sold his horseradish in clear bottles. He proudly showed his customers that his horseradish contained *only* horseradish.

His experience selling horseradish taught Henry two important lessons. Some people were willing to pay for prepared food, rather than make it themselves. And they would pay a little more for the best-quality ingredients. Henry was ready to provide both.

CHAPTER 2
Early Success

Henry John Heinz seemed to work almost nonstop, between his father's brick business and his own food sales. In 1861, Henry sold $2,400—about $65,000 in today's money—worth of produce and his ever-popular horseradish. Not too bad for a seventeen-year-old!

During his teen years, Henry learned how to preserve food—bottling it in jars so it wouldn't spoil. German families like the Heinzes usually had their own recipes for making sauerkraut, horseradish, and pickles at home. Henry's mother taught him her recipes for pickling. While horseradish remained his main product, Henry later gained fame for his pickles, as well. Mrs. Heinz also taught him that he should treat all people as he would want to be treated. His mother's recipes and beliefs shaped Henry's growing business.

While Henry learned valuable lessons from his mother, he also stayed busy with his father's brickmaking business. In 1866, Henry became a partner in his father's company and quickly made changes. At the time, most brickyards shut down for the winter. Henry decided to heat the small factory so it could stay open through the cold months. That way, the company would have a supply of bricks ready when the demand for bricks rose in the spring.

Henry was good at the business of making and selling bricks. But his real passion was preparing and selling horseradish, and he wanted to do more of it. In 1869, he and his friend L. Clarence Noble started a company that sold horseradish with the brand name Anchor. For Henry, an anchor stood for something that was solid and could be trusted. That's how he wanted people to feel about his product. As he had before, Henry packaged the horseradish in a glass bottle, so customers could see exactly what they were buying.

The Anchor name and the clear glass bottles were just two of Henry's efforts to market his products. Marketing is how a company decides to price, distribute, sell, and promote its products. And Henry wanted to be as good at marketing as he was at raising crops, pickling them, and packaging them for sale. As before, using the glass bottles highlighted Henry's obsession with quality. And choosing a strong name would create a positive image in the customer's mind.

Henry now devoted all his time to growing crops, perfecting recipes, and packaging his foods for sale. His company started out in the basement of the Heinzes' Sharpsburg home but quickly grew. It expanded into the entire house, and then the Anchor company bought the house next door!

Pittsburgh, Pennsylvania, circa 1869

The region around Pittsburgh was booming, too. Oil had been discovered nearby. And the city produced more glass than any other in the world. New businesses, iron mills, and factories meant that more workers flocked to Pittsburgh. The increasing population needed to eat, and Heinz and Noble were determined to feed them.

Henry also wanted to expand his business beyond Pennsylvania, so he used trains to ship his products to new markets and to personally meet with salesmen and customers in a growing number of states. Whenever a new rail route opened up between Pittsburgh and another city, Henry would hop on the train, looking for new business opportunities. He even carried notebooks filled with information on the train schedules.

Expansion of the Railroads

H. J. Heinz was only eight years old when people in Pittsburgh saw the arrival of the first train from Philadelphia in 1852. Railroads were still fairly new in the United States, but they were growing quickly.

By 1868, companies in and around Pittsburgh provided iron and steel to build trains and rails, and coal to power engines. Trains carried all sorts of supplies from the East Coast through Pittsburgh and across the United States. Just a year later, two railroad companies finished building the first railroad that linked the East and West Coasts of the United States.

In 1869, Henry married Sarah Young. Her family had come to America from Ireland, where they had owned a mill. Heinz called his new wife Sallie. Over the next few years, Sallie watched her husband and his partner put the Anchor name on more products: pickles, sauces, and even their own vinegar. Because vinegar was the main ingredient in many Anchor condiments, it made sense for the two men to manufacture and sell their own.

In 1872, Heinz and Noble made Noble's brother E. J. a partner, and they renamed the business Heinz, Noble & Company. The company expanded into Pittsburgh and included a factory, warehouse, and office space.

As Henry's company grew, so did his family. Sallie and Henry had a daughter, Irene, in 1871, and two years later, a boy named Clarence. The family still lived in Sharpsburg, and Henry took the train back and forth to Pittsburgh for work.

At the factory, he kept a close eye on the young women who washed bottles to make sure they didn't break them. He encouraged workers to give up smoking cigarettes and drinking. When Henry got home from the factory, he often continued working, doing bookkeeping and writing business letters until late at night. His hard work and strict standards paid off.

By the beginning of 1875, Heinz, Noble & Company had grown tremendously. It grew its own vegetables on 160 acres of land in and around Sharpsburg. It opened a factory in St. Louis, Missouri, to make its own vinegar. And it

maintained a warehouse stocked with products in Chicago. A magazine reviewing Pennsylvania companies at the time marveled at how quickly the company had grown. The writer noted that Henry's company sold only "first class" products. The future looked bright for Henry and his partners.

What Is a Condiment?

A condiment is something that is added to food to give it more flavor or to improve the taste. Condiments are never the main course, but they can certainly make a meal!

Some of the most popular condiments are ketchup, mustard, relish, salsa, hot sauce, and soy sauce.

CHAPTER 3
Starting Over

While Heinz, Noble & Company did well during the early 1870s, the United States as a whole was facing a business crisis. In 1873, the country entered what is called a depression—a period in which many companies slow down production and lose money, forcing them to cut back on workers or shut down completely. Many people who were out of work looked to the banks for loans. But as the companies struggled, banks often stopped making loans.

By 1875, Henry saw that his company faced disaster, too. It owed more money than it could afford to pay back. He wrote in his diary in April that he "could eat no dinner owing to worry and hurry and planning."

Henry turned to his father and a friendly

local banker who loaned him the money to pay some of the company's bills. Even his wife, Sallie, pitched in, giving Henry some of her own money. Still, the company went deeper into debt, and by the year's end it went bankrupt—it shut down for good because it could not pay the money it owed.

Henry felt that most of the businesspeople he knew had abandoned him. "I feel very sad," he wrote, "as though I had not a true friend in the world." The Noble brothers seemed to blame Henry for the company's struggles. They refused to invest any more of their own money. Henry's family, though, stuck by his side. He also had his deep faith in God to help him get through the tough times. He was not going to give up. He would not leave the business he loved.

On New Year's Day 1876, Henry asked his family to help him start a new business. His brother John and his cousin Frederick agreed, and Sallie once again provided some of her own money. Because his first company had gone bankrupt, Henry could not legally be a part owner of this new one. Instead, he was just another worker, paid $125 a month. But the family understood that the new F. & J. Heinz Company was really Henry's. He had the business skills and the right contacts in the food business. And he would do the hard work needed to make people trust the Heinz name once again.

The whole family pitched in. His mother and sisters bottled horseradish in the basement of their home, just as Henry had done years before. With his new company, Henry also introduced a brand-new product. Ketchup, also spelled catsup, had been popular

for several decades in the United States. Like preparing horseradish, making ketchup at home was hard work. It took a full day to make one batch. So Henry told his customers that buying his product, instead of making their own, would save them a lot of time.

Ketchup!

Americans love their ketchup, but the first sauces with that name came from Vietnam and China. The word *ketchup* comes from a Chinese word, *kê-tsiap*, which is a type of fish sauce. Perhaps as early as the late 1600s, British traders in Asia tasted the local *kê-tsiap* and tried to re-create it at home. The Asian sauces had contained fish, and British recipes included such things as walnuts, mushrooms, and oysters. They were nothing like the tomato ketchup that Henry J. Heinz's company made famous.

Tomatoes first appeared in ketchup in the 1800s. The version we know today—tomatoes, vinegar, sugar, spices, and salt—was first sold in 1876.

Thanks to Henry's hard work, the new company was growing and making money. His success must have been a comfort when Sallie and Henry had their third child in August 1877. They named their son Howard. Soon after, Henry rented a house for the growing family near the company's Pittsburgh factory.

As the F. & J. Heinz Company grew, Henry fulfilled a promise he had made to himself when he started it. He would pay back his share of the debt that he and the Nobles still hadn't repaid. He considered it his duty. Paying all the money he owed also helped regain the trust of banks. With that trust restored and quality condiments to sell, Henry's company was ready to keep growing.

CHAPTER 4
Seeds of Success

Building a successful company was hard work, but Henry had been working hard since he was a boy. He was not going to slow down now. And even as he tested new recipes, traveled,

and watched over his workers, Henry found time to keep a diary. He described details of his work and family life. After inviting his employees to his home for dinner one night, he wrote in his diary that "all learned much and were highly entertained and amused."

Early in 1879, Henry, Sallie, and their children left their rented house in Pittsburgh and moved back to Sharpsburg. Henry played an active role in his church there, and he was especially dedicated to the idea of Sunday schools. While their parents went to church services, children attended classes to learn about the Bible and their Christian faith.

Henry viewed religion classes as a great way to teach children about God and help them to become better people. Henry himself was known for his generous ways. Poor men could count on him for a meal, and he sometimes loaned money to his customers so they could stay in business.

Along with keeping a diary, Henry also kept a recipe book. And although he still used his mother's horseradish recipe, he also created  recipes of his own. Most he kept secret or wrote down in code. Only his relatives at the company knew the full recipes.

At times, Henry also tried to copy recipes from his competitors. One of the foods that Henry tried to imitate was called chowchow, a combination of cauliflower and other pickled vegetables in a mustard and vinegar sauce. But when copying chowchow or other condiments, Henry made his version stand out by offering the highest-quality food.

When not tinkering with recipes, Henry developed ways to make his products more convenient. For example, customers usually had to buy vinegar out of a large barrel at the local store. Henry began selling his vinegar in smaller bottles that were easier to carry home and keep on the shelf. People in Pittsburgh knew Henry as "the pickle man," even though he was now selling a large variety of foods, including jelly, apple butter, and chili sauce. Henry also wanted to

provide customers with unusual condiments they couldn't find anywhere else, like Asian quince jelly.

In 1880, the company had its most successful year ever. In Pittsburgh, people saw teams of horses pulling wagons carrying Heinz products, and the company name was always printed on the side. Grocery stores boasted in their ads that they carried the popular Heinz brand. Henry also sent his salesmen to fairs and other public events to offer free samples. Henry was sure that once people tasted Heinz products, they would look for them in their own stores.

Along with a growing business, Henry also had a growing family. His son Clifford was born in 1883. While Henry loved his family, traveling for work meant he spent a lot of time away from Sallie and the children. In 1884, he traveled by train to Chicago, where the company had an office, and as far south as Florida. On his trips,

he met with customers and gave pep talks to his sales force. He even tried to think up ways to get his salesmen excited about selling vinegar! But Henry never had trouble getting excited about his products. He was as confident as he had been as a young boy selling fresh vegetables.

Still, Henry did make time to focus on his family and their Sharpsburg home. He had a keen interest in new technology, and the telephone was the latest thing. It had been perfected by Alexander Graham Bell in 1876, and the first one appeared in Pittsburgh in 1878. Three years later, Henry had a phone line hung between his house and the house where his mother lived.

In 1886, the Heinzes took a family vacation, to visit Henry's parents' homeland of Germany. They set off by train from Pittsburgh to New Jersey, then they boarded an ocean liner and sailed across the Atlantic Ocean. Their first stop was England. Henry brought samples of some of his best products and visited a company in London that sold groceries. To his delight, the company agreed to sell Heinz ketchup, horseradish, and other products that Henry would ship from the United States.

As the trip went on, Henry visited different factories to see how European manufacturers processed their own products. In Germany, he visited the house where his father had lived as a boy. When the trip was over, Henry returned to Pittsburgh with many new ideas for his own factories. He had taken his first step toward running a global company.

CHAPTER 5
Building a Modern Company

By 1887, Henry Heinz had taken the small business he started with his family eleven years earlier and turned it into a food-producing giant.

Things did not always run smoothly, though, between Henry and his younger brother John. John was not as dedicated to the business as Henry was. In August 1888, the family held a meeting and John decided to sell his part of the company. Henry's cousin Frederick, who was also a part owner, had already sold some of his share back to Henry. Now Sallie and Henry owned a little more than half of the company, which was renamed the H. J. Heinz Company.

With a new name for his company, Henry also wanted a new factory. He hoped to adapt some of the business methods he had observed in Germany. There, he had seen the Stollwerck chocolate factory use steam-powered machines to do some of the work that used to be done by hand. The machines completed the work much faster.

Henry also saw how the Stollwerck company helped its workers. The factory had a lunchroom

Stollwerck chocolate factory

and a store for its employees. And the company established schools for their children. Outside of work hours, the company held picnics and dinners, and it gave employees their own small plots of land to farm. The company even helped find doctors for workers who got sick.

Henry had always treated his workers fairly,
but this German system was unlike anything he
had seen in the United States. And Henry realized
its value. Happy, well-cared-for employees would
stay on the job and work hard. They would not
be interested in causing trouble for their bosses.

Henry had seen firsthand the violence that could occur when workers and company owners fought. In 1877, some US railroad companies had cut workers' wages. Angry workers then walked off their jobs—they went on strike. In Pittsburgh, the striking workers and their supporters clashed with National Guard troops, leaving more than twenty people dead. Henry hated the violence and did not want his workers to feel that he did not care for them.

Pittsburgh railroad strike of 1877

In 1889, he bought land in Allegheny City, just outside Pittsburgh. The site offered easy access to the Allegheny River and to railroad lines. He quickly began building the first of several buildings that would become part of a huge factory complex. Henry had a railway built right into the plant so trains could easily bring in

produce and take out packaged food. The work on the new factory continued for nearly ten years. Eventually, the factory site included a restaurant, an indoor pool, an emergency room for medical issues, and an auditorium, where workers went to hear concerts and lectures.

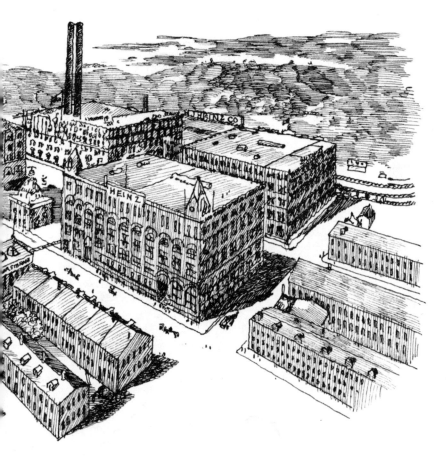

Henry hired more workers—and more women. They bottled pickles, trimmed meat, and peeled fruit. Male and female employees had separate dressing rooms with bathrooms, at a time when many people did not have indoor toilets in their own homes. The women also received freshly washed uniforms each day. The company offered classes in English and other subjects for anyone who did not speak English or who had not completed their education.

Henry treated his growing number of horses well, too. More than one hundred horses lived in a three-story stable. The company kept its wagons on the first floor, while the horses lived on the second, and supplies were stored on the third. Henry's stable was so modern, it used electric machines to feed, water, and brush the horses. They even had their own hospital and warm baths where they could soak their tired feet!

Henry also installed the most modern
machinery in his factory. Moving belts carried
the food and the bottles along each step of the
process. This was an early form of what was later
called mass production.

As his business expanded and improved, Henry decided to buy a huge new house in the Point Breeze neighborhood of Pittsburgh. The most successful business owners in the city lived there. The new Heinz home was called Greenlawn.

Greenlawn

Mass Production

American manufacturers of the nineteenth century constantly looked for ways to make their products faster and cheaper.

In 1913, Henry Ford perfected mass production with his Model T car. Parts moved through the factory

and workers performed the same task over and over, working on what was called the production line. The year before his employees began assembling cars on the production line, Ford made about 69,000 cars. But only one year later, in 1914, the company produced more than 202,000 Model T Fords!

Millionaires' Row

The city of Pittsburgh had continued to see its industries grow since the 1870s, and the wealthy men who founded factories and banks lived near each other in a neighborhood called "Millionaires' Row." They included electrical industry pioneer George Westinghouse; Andrew Carnegie, head of the largest steel company in the world; and his friend Henry Clay Frick. Their homes in Millionaires' Row were large and elegant estates. The neighborhood even had its own private station on the railroad line!

Henry, Sallie, and their four children had plenty of space in Greenlawn's thirty rooms spread out over four floors. Henry installed colorful stained glass in several rooms and turned the upper floor into his own personal museum.

He displayed the art and objects he had collected on his business trips. Outside, the Heinz children rode their own ponies while Henry spent time in the ten greenhouses on the grounds. Just as when he was a boy, he continued to work with the soil,

planting fruit trees and vegetables, as well as rare flowers. In April 1892, Henry said, "We are all much delighted with our new home."

Henry had much to be proud of. In 1892, he opened his first major factory outside Pittsburgh—a sauerkraut factory in Muscatine, Iowa. The company had branch offices and warehouses in a number of cities across the United States. It even had small salting stations to begin the pickling of cucumbers as they were picked in the fields.

Michigan salting station

In 1893, Henry made a splash at the Columbian Exposition, a huge fair held in Chicago to celebrate the four hundredth anniversary of Christopher Columbus's arrival in the New World.

The World's Columbian Exposition of 1893

Over the course of six months, more than twenty-five million people attended the Columbian Exposition in Chicago, Illinois. George Westinghouse provided the electricity to power the more than two hundred thousand lightbulbs that illuminated the fair. The exhibit featured the world's first Ferris wheel, a 250-foot-tall machine that could carry more than two thousand people at a time. And thousands of companies introduced their new products to visitors, such as Aunt Jemima's pancake mix and Juicy Fruit chewing gum.

For the exposition, Henry had designed a pin in the shape of a pickle with the company name on it. At the fair, people flocked to the Heinz exhibit on the second floor to get a free pickle pin. So many people wanted the pins that the second floor of the building began to sag! Other business owners quickly saw the value of handing out small items to promote their company name. Once again, Henry's good idea had proven to be a winner, and his company gave away pickle pins for more than one hundred years.

CHAPTER 6
"57 Varieties" and Many More

After the excitement of the Columbian Exposition, Henry decided that he needed a vacation. Early in 1894, he went to Europe, Egypt, and the Middle East. Henry, who was nearly fifty, traveled with two of his children and a niece. Sallie, who had not been feeling well, stayed home.

Henry played tourist among the famous pyramids of Egypt, and he bought souvenirs to send home. But he couldn't seem to stay away from work. In Germany, he took orders from a new customer. And when he returned to Pittsburgh, Henry threw himself right back into his work. He set out on a US tour of his factories and rural salting stations.

The end of 1894, however, brought great sadness to the Heinz family. Henry's wife, Sallie, was still sick. Her temperature rose, and she

developed pneumonia, a lung disease. Henry prayed for Sallie's recovery, but on Thanksgiving night, she died. The day of her funeral, Henry wrote, was "the darkest day we ever knew."

To take his mind off his sorrows, Henry focused on the company. The country was once again going through hard economic times, as it had during the 1870s. But by this time, Henry was one of the country's wealthiest people. The H. J. Heinz Company increased its profits every year, as new plants equipped with machines helped cut the costs of producing Heinz-brand foods. Henry also continuously added new products, such as canned baked beans and soups.

During the last few years of the 1890s, Henry repeatedly showed his genius for promoting the Heinz name. While visiting New York City in 1896, he saw a sign advertising "21 styles of shoes." He thought of the many different foods he sold. He knew there were more than sixty. But for some reason, he thought the number fifty-seven sounded *right*. Instantly, Henry knew he had a new slogan for his company: "Heinz 57 Varieties." He later wrote, "Within a week, the sign of the green pickle with the '57 Varieties' was appearing in newspapers, on billboards, signboards, and

everywhere else I could find a place to stick it." The phrase "Heinz 57" was even spelled out in concrete blocks on several hills across the country.

Henry, though, didn't want people to merely see his company name and slogan. He wanted them to learn just how special his foods were, and to give people a fun way to sample them. In 1898, he bought a pier in Atlantic City, New Jersey.

The city on the Atlantic Ocean drew visitors to its beach and the famous wooden boardwalk built on top of it. Henry's pier jutted out almost nine hundred feet from the boardwalk into the ocean. At the near end of the pier was a building where tourists could sit and read magazines or newspapers while surrounded by samples of Heinz products. The rooms were also decorated with art.

At the far end of the pier sat a larger building with huge windows that looked over the ocean. It had a hall where visitors listened to talks about the Heinz Company and its many operations. Tourists could even place orders for Heinz foods that would be delivered to their homes. During the summer, fifteen thousand people might visit the Heinz Pier each day! Even people who didn't walk out onto the pier couldn't miss the huge electric sign that sat on top of the larger building. It said simply: "57."

Tourists who came to Pittsburgh could see the Heinz factory in operation for themselves. Among US industrialists—the men who built large, modern factories—Henry was the first to open up his plant to visitors. He wanted people to see how clean and modern the factory was so they would know they were getting the best food possible. Visitors got to taste samples and received a Heinz pickle pin. By 1900, twenty thousand visitors took the factory tour each year.

That year, Henry continued to show his flair for advertising and his interest in the latest technology. He erected the first electric sign in New York City! More than one thousand lights

flashed an ad for his Atlantic City pier, along with his famous "57 Varieties" slogan. Henry was also the first person to use electric streetcars in the city of Pittsburgh. And like the horse-drawn wagons and railroad cars his company used, they proudly displayed the Heinz name.

At the dawn of the twentieth century, the H. J. Heinz Company was the largest food processing company in the United States. It sold more than two hundred products, and people across the country knew and trusted the Heinz brand name.

Henry owned a glass plant in Sharpsburg that

manufactured bottles, and a Pittsburgh plant that made the company's own boxes, barrels, and cans. More than twenty thousand people helped harvest crops, and another 2,800 people worked for the company year-round. Henry could not have imagined creating a company this size when he was first making horseradish in the family basement! But now he was the head of a food empire.

CHAPTER 7
The Fight for Pure Food

In 1900, Howard Heinz graduated from Yale University, where he had studied chemistry. And he went right to work at the H. J. Heinz Company. He was in charge of part of the pickle production. Howard was already a part owner of the company.

Henry was still actively involved in the family business, of course. He played a big role in addressing a major concern of the day: food purity. He knew from his early days selling horseradish that some companies sometimes tried to save money by adding nonfood ingredients into their recipes.

By 1900, manufacturers were also adding chemicals to some of their products. The chemicals could give foods a certain color that customers found appealing, such as bright green pickles. Others helped preserve food so it didn't spoil. But in some cases, the chemicals could be harmful.

With his son Howard and his brother-in-law Sebastian Mueller, Henry joined the fight to establish food purity laws. They wanted to prevent companies from adding

Sebastian Mueller

harmful chemicals to their foods. While Henry had always taken pride in making his foods as pure as possible, he knew other companies didn't. Henry wanted to build trust and make sure customers got the best-quality, best-tasting foods possible.

Henry knew that simple ingredients like salt and vinegar could help stop foods from spoiling. He used as few chemical preservatives as possible in his food.

In 1906, H. J. Heinz was the first food company to make ketchup without chemical preservatives.

To keep the ketchup fresh, the company used only the ripest tomatoes and vinegar as a natural preservative. It also made sure the bottles were thoroughly cleaned before the ketchup went in.

In 1905, Henry sent Howard and Sebastian to Washington, DC, to meet with President Theodore Roosevelt. Unlike many presidents before him, Roosevelt was willing to use the power of the government to help stop harmful

Theodore Roosevelt

business practices. At first, the president was not sure that national laws to control how foods were processed and labeled were needed. Still, the H. J. Heinz Company and a few other businesses were anxious to have a law passed.

Then, in 1906, Roosevelt and many Americans read a book called *The Jungle*. Its author, Upton Sinclair, described the unhealthy conditions in Chicago meatpacking plants. The book convinced many people that Henry was right—the country needed food purity laws. Congress passed the Pure Food and Drug Act, and President Roosevelt signed it into law on June 30, 1906.

By this time, Henry was letting Howard and Sebastian Mueller run more of the company's daily operations. He spent more time on his own projects in Pittsburgh. One of them was to make Allegheny City, site of his factory, an official part of the city of Pittsburgh. The move would make Pittsburgh one of the largest cities in the country,

The Jungle

When Upton Sinclair sat down to write *The Jungle*, he wanted to show Americans the difficulties immigrants faced in their new country. He had spent several weeks visiting meatpacking plants and interviewing the workers. Sinclair thought the factory owners treated the immigrant workers horribly. The owners didn't care if their employees were injured on the job or didn't earn enough money to support their families.

But when *The Jungle* was published in 1906, many readers were astounded—not by the treatment of the immigrants, but by the terrible conditions Sinclair described in the meatpacking plants. Americans realized that the food they were eating might be unsafe. And they wanted the government to force companies to sell only pure food.

and Henry thought that would make the residents proud. The two communities merged in 1906.

Promoting Sunday school and helping others remained a key part of Henry's life. He worked

with different organizations that tried to spread Sunday schools across the country and around the world. But while he kept busy with his many interests, Henry also found some time to relax.

He began playing golf. And at age sixty-seven, he showed a still-growing sense of adventure. In 1911, Henry was just the fifth passenger ever on the world's first flying boat. This plane could take off and land on water. "I want to keep ahead of my boys," he said after. "I don't want them to do anything I can do first."

Also that year, he returned to Europe and Egypt, buying art and other items along the way. He particularly liked old watches and pieces of carved ivory. But even on this trip, he took time for business. In London, he visited a Heinz factory.

Henry was proud of the hard work the company had done to become so successful there.

Two years later, at almost seventy years old, Henry took a six-month trip around the world. Along with his son Clarence and other people who wanted to promote the idea of Sunday schools, he visited China, Japan, and Korea. The group then traveled by train across Russia. Henry's faith inspired his hard work for the Sunday school mission and his desire to help others. In 1913, he donated money to build a center for the poor children of Pittsburgh. It featured a gym, a swimming pool, and classrooms. Henry named it the Sarah Heinz House, in honor of his wife.

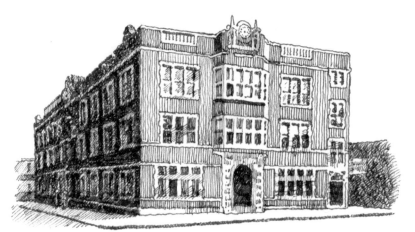

CHAPTER 8
Final Years

In the summer of 1914, Henry was once again traveling in Europe. At the beginning of August, Germany declared war on Russia and France. Soon those countries and many more were fighting what came to be called World War I. Henry and other Americans who were staying at a German spa heard little news about the war.

They were not even sure when they would be able to return home. Finally, after several weeks, Henry was allowed to return to America.

The war dragged on for several years. During that time, Henry saw sales rise throughout Europe as foreign governments bought Heinz pickles and

baked beans for their troops. But the fighting prevented Henry from going back to Europe. Instead, he spent his time closer to home. His private museum at Greenlawn was now open to the public, and schoolchildren often visited to see his collections of watches and art.

Visitors to Greenlawn also included Henry's own grandchildren. By now, both Irene and Howard had children, and Henry sometimes played with them or took them on short drives. Howard Heinz was now firmly in control of the company, though Henry still visited the factory and offered his opinions on how it should be run.

If anyone thought Henry was slowing down, he proved them wrong on his seventy-first birthday.

When asked how he felt for his age, Henry jumped over a chair! He was still traveling and visiting friends and family. And he continued to meet with Heinz salesmen and farmers across the country.

In April 1917, the United States entered World War I. Howard took a job with the state of Pennsylvania, which left him little time to work at the Heinz Company. Each state in the United States tried to convince its residents to grow their own food. The government wanted to make sure it had enough food to feed US soldiers, as well as the nations it was helping in Europe.

The war ended in November 1918. To celebrate, workers at the Heinz Company shut down the plant. Some drove the Heinz trucks in a parade through the streets of Pittsburgh. Neither Howard nor Henry seemed to mind one bit.

Howard left his job with the state of Pennsylvania and took a job with the US government. He helped to provide food to people in Europe and the Middle East. Howard spent five months out of the country before returning to take control of the H. J. Heinz Company again.

Howard's wife, Betty, kept a close watch on Henry. He still enjoyed golf and traveling, and in March 1919, Betty wrote to Howard that Henry was looking well. But in May, he became ill. What seemed to be a cold was actually pneumonia. On May 14, Henry John Heinz died at Greenlawn.

The Heinz Mausoleum in Homewood Cemetery, Pittsburgh

Henry died a multimillionaire. He left much of his wealth and his collections to his children and to his brothers and sisters. He also gave money to Sunday school associations, his Sharpsburg church, a college, and three hospitals.

More important than money, though, was the business Henry left behind. The H. J. Heinz Company was still run by his son Howard. It would continue to grow, thanks to the ideas Henry had always believed in: Work hard and offer the best products possible.

Over the years, the Heinz Company continued to innovate. In 1968, it was the first company to offer ketchup in small "to-go" packets. In 1983, Heinz introduced the first squeezable plastic bottle for ketchup. Today, the company sells more than 650 million bottles of ketchup every year!

In 2015, the H. J. Heinz Company merged with Kraft, another well-known US food manufacturer. Henry's name lives on in the new

Kraft Heinz Company that employs people in forty different countries. At the time of the merger, it was the fifth-largest food company in the world.

Henry's impact on the modern food industry lives on, too. His idea to show off his ingredients in clear bottles won him many loyal customers. His talent for clever advertising and marketing brought him even more. Perhaps most important, Henry John Heinz believed in quality. And he oversaw that quality in all aspects of his business. The Heinz legacy continues to this day.

Timeline of H. J. Heinz's Life

1844 — Born on October 11 in Birmingham, Pennsylvania

1869 — Starts a food business with L. Clarence Noble

— Marries Sarah "Sallie" Young

1871 — Has a daughter named Irene

1873 — Has a son named Clarence

1875 — Heinz, Noble & Company goes bankrupt

1876 — Starts F. & J. Heinz Company with his family and begins selling ketchup for the first time

1877 — Has a son named Howard

1883 — Has a son named Clifford

1886 — Visits Europe with family and makes first foreign sales

1888 — Takes control of the F. & J. Heinz Company and renames it the H. J. Heinz Company

1892 — Buys Greenlawn

1893 — Attracts thousands of visitors to his exhibit at the Columbian Exposition by giving away Heinz pickle pins

1896 — Creates the "57 Varieties" slogan

1898 — Buys a pier in Atlantic City to promote his products

1906 — Welcomes the passing of the Pure Food and Drug Act, which he had strongly supported

1913 — Travels to promote the Sunday school movement

1919 — Dies at Greenlawn on May 14

Timeline of the World

1848 — James W. Marshall finds gold at Sutter's Mill, in Coloma, California, which begins the California gold rush

1861 — The Civil War begins in South Carolina

1865 — The Civil War ends

— President Abraham Lincoln is assassinated

1867 — Alfred Nobel invents dynamite

1869 — Railways connect the East and West Coasts of the United States for the first time

1880 — Thomas Edison receives a patent for the lightbulb

1886 — German inventor Karl Benz receives a patent for the automobile

1887 — Sir Arthur Conan Doyle publishes his first story about Sherlock Holmes

1893 — New Zealand becomes the first country to give women the right to vote

1906 — In San Francisco, an earthquake and the fires that follow kill more than three thousand people

1908 — Henry Ford makes his first Model T car

1912 — The British ship *Titanic* hits an iceberg and sinks

1914 — World War I begins

1918 — World War I ends

Bibliography

*Books for young readers

Alberts, Robert C. *The Good Provider: H. J. Heinz and His 57 Varieties.* Boston: Houghton Mifflin, 1973.

*Bliss, John. *Processing Your Food.* Chicago: Heinemann Library, 2012.

*Burgan, Michael. *Who Was Henry Ford?* New York: Penguin Workshop, 2014.

D'Costa, Krystal. "Seeing Is Believing: The Story Behind Henry Heinz's Condiment Empire." *Scientific American*, March 26, 2012. http://blogs.scientificamerican.com/anthropology-in-practice/seeing-is-believing-the-story-behind-henry-heinzs-condiment-empire/.

Foster, Debbie, and Jack Kennedy. *H. J. Heinz Company.* Charleston, SC: Arcadia Publishing, 2006.

*James, Dawn. *Turning Tomatoes into Ketchup.* New York: Cavendish Square Publishing, 2014.

Koehn, Nancy Fowler. *Brand New: How Entrepreneurs Earned Consumers' Trust from Wedgwood to Dell.* Boston: Harvard Business School Press, 2001.

Lentz, Steve. *It Was Never About the Ketchup!: The Life and Leadership Secrets of H. J. Heinz.* New York: Morgan James Publishing, 2007.

Skrabec Jr., Quentin R. *H. J. Heinz: A Biography.* Jefferson, NC: McFarland & Company, 2009.

Smith, Andrew F. *Pure Ketchup: A History of America's National Condiment, With Recipes.* Columbia, SC: University of South Carolina Press, 1996.